TRAN BOOKS

Trung Nguyen Coffee

Thirty Years of a Name, 1996–2026

Counted. Not Claimed.

CALVIN P. TRAN

Every story of a beginning is told after the ending is known.

The people who were there did not know it yet, and that is the only honest place to start.

—Calvin P. Tran

TRUNG NGUYÊN COFFEE

Thirty Years of a Name, 1996–2026

By Calvin P. Tran

This book records a name being made.
Within it, what a company announces and what the record confirms are set side by side — and neither is asked to yield.

Tran Books
World Trade Center Long Beach, California 90831
www.tranbooks.com

For rights, permissions, bulk orders, and special sales inquiries:
publication@tranbooks.com

First Tran Books paperback edition, September 2026
Tran Books Publication and its logo are trademarks of UIMEX, LLC.

Counted. Not Claimed.

Library of Congress Control Number: 2026921623
ISBN: 979-8-9958530-6-0 (Paperback)

Also available as an eBook.

Also by

TRAN BOOKS

WORLD: Fracture Lines

Writing. Responsibility.

The world rarely changes all at once.
More often, it changes through fractures.

Library of Congress Control Number: 2026918722
ISBN: 979-8-9958530-7-7 | Also available as an eBook.

Trump, a Curious Tale

Record. Not Judge.

On spectacle, power, and the emotional architecture of modern politics.

Library of Congress Control Number: 2026903064
ISBN: 979-8-9958530-0-8 | Also available as an eBook.

Trump, Kỳ truyện

Record. Not Judge.

On spectacle, power, and the emotional architecture of modern politics.

Library of Congress Control Number: 2026903064
ISBN: 979-8-9958530-1-5 | Also available as an eBook.

Night 1002 — The Persian Dawn

Witness. Write. Endure.

Where empires continue speaking
after history believes the story has ended.

Library of Congress Control Number: 2026910703
ISBN: 979-8-9958530-2-2 | Also available as an eBook.

AMERICA: *The Stillness*

Silence. Records.

A chronicle written through silence rather than declaration.

Library of Congress Control Number: 2026913471
ISBN: 979-8-9958530-8-4 | Also available as an eBook.

Where Havana Goes

Asked. Not Answered.

Ninety miles, and one hundred twenty-eight years, 1898–2026.

Library of Congress Control Number: 2026923022
ISBN: 979-8-9977742-1-9 | Also available as an eBook.

Musk & Trump

Dated. Not Decided.

Didn't Need Each Other. Needed Each Other. Tore Into Each Other. Shook Hands Again.

Library of Congress Control Number: 2026923090
ISBN: 979-8-9977742-2-6 | Also available as an eBook.

Trung Nguyen Coffee

Counted. Not Claimed.

Thirty Years of a Name, 1996–2026

Library of Congress Control Number: 2026921623
ISBN: 979-8-9958530-6-0 | Also available as an eBook.

Amazon: amazon.com/author/calvinptran

Goodreads: goodreads.com/tranbooks

Publisher: tranbooks.com

TABLE OF CONTENTS

PART TWO

PART THREE

Trung Nguyen Coffee

Thirty Years of a Name, 1996–2026

Counted. Not Claimed.

PREFACE

There is a road one hundred fifty-one kilometers long that joins the sea to the highlands, and this book begins there.

A reader picks the book up because of a name. That name appears on packaging in more than sixty countries, on signboards in Buon Ma Thuot, in Saigon, in Shanghai, and for the past few years on a street in Southern California where Vietnamese people have lived for fifty years. The story behind the name has been told many times, usually in very large letters.

This book takes another route.

What is recorded here is what can be counted. One hand-cranked roasting drum set over a wood fire. A few kilos of green coffee taken on credit and paid for later. A roasting formula given away by a woman whose name no source has yet recorded. Two hundred million dong borrowed from a family nobody can name either. The friends who signed a business application in 1996, then vanished from the file in 2000. An address on Nguyen Kiem Street, and ten days of free coffee.

These things are small, and because they are small they can be used again.

The later part of the story cannot be repeated by anyone. Nobody can hold the 2003 blind tasting again in the circumstances in which it was held, or reach the nine thousand five hundred sales points announced as a target in 2006, or the hundred million books announced for a giveaway program. But taking delivery of a few kilos and paying on the day you said you would — anyone can do that, in any trade, in any year. If this book is of use to some young person, the useful part is in the early chapters and not the later ones.

The book also does not hide what it does not know.

The year he entered university appears as three different figures in three different sources. The business has two birthdays sixty days apart. The number of shops in the United States has one figure that was announced and one that can be counted, and the two do not match. In places like these, the book sets the facts side by side and stops, rather than choosing whichever version sounds smoother.

The person who wrote this book does not call himself an author. What has been done here is recording: reading what remains, arranging it in order of time, leaving the disagreements where they are, and adding nothing that is not in the file.

Thirty years is a round number. History is not round like that.

The Recorder, *September 2026*

A NOTE ON SOURCES AND METHOD

This book was written under a set of fixed rules. A reader who knows the rules in advance will read it correctly.

On sources.

The material comes from five kinds of document: Vietnamese press reporting from 2004 through August 2026; legal texts and business-registration records as quoted in the press; material and statements issued by the company itself; testimony given by the parties at the 2019 hearing, as reported; and Mr. Dang Le Nguyen Vu's own account given in interviews. These five are not equally reliable, and the book does not blend them into one.

On what the recorder saw.

In a few places the recorder went to the place himself and set down what he found there. Those passages say so plainly. They are observation, not document, and they are marked as such wherever they appear.

An account is not a fact.
Where a detail exists only in the account of someone involved, the sentence says so. Where a figure was announced by the company, the sentence says so. That a statement was reprinted by many newspapers does not make it many sources: dozens of articles carrying the same press release remain one source.

Not yet found is different from does not exist.
In many places the document that ought to exist has not been located. The book records that, without concluding that no such document exists.

Disagreements are left standing.
Where two sources give two figures, the book chooses neither. Both are set side by side, with their provenance. Where three sources give three figures, the sentence keeps only what all three agree on, unless the disagreement is itself worth recording, in which case all three are given.

No dialogue is invented.

Not one line of speech in this book has been placed in the mouth of a real person. No thought, motive, or feeling is attributed to anyone who did not state it personally. In a few places the general setting of a region in a given year is reconstructed from documents about that region; such passages describe a place, not a particular day in a particular life.

On the legal dispute.

The years 2015–2021 are recorded by dates and the names of documents, and no more. The book does not narrate the proceedings, does not set out either side's arguments, and does not comment on the rulings.

On money.

Every sum is given in the value of its own time, with no conversion to present-day terms. Every target, projection, or announced figure is dated to the moment it was stated.

On place names.

Buon Ma Thuot was raised from town to city on

January 21, 1995. Chapters set before that date use town. The district name is written without diacritics as M'Drak; the Vietnamese form is M'Đrắk.

On diacritics.

Vietnamese words appear in this edition without diacritical marks: Buon Ma Thuot, M'Drak, Trung Nguyen. The Vietnamese forms are Buôn Ma Thuột, M'Đrắk, Trung Nguyên.

Proper names of businesses, publications, and pen names keep their original form.

A note on figures in this edition.

Numerals are used for statistics, dates, and sums. Small counts inside the narrative are spelled out, as they are in the Vietnamese edition.

DISCLAIMER

This book is an independent work of record. It is not commissioned, sponsored, authorized, or approved by Mr. Dang Le Nguyen Vu, by Trung Nguyen Group, Trung Nguyen Legend, or by any individual or company named in it. The writer has no ownership, employment, or consulting relationship with any of them.

Trademarks, trade names, and product names appearing in this book belong to their owners and are used here for purposes of reporting and commentary only.

The contents are based on publicly available material obtained through August 2026. The writer has tried to verify every detail but makes no warranty as to the completeness or absolute accuracy of any of it, and accepts no responsibility for errors, omissions, or the consequences of relying on the text. Many details here come from accounts recorded years after the events, and human memory is not a file.

Nothing here is offered as investment, business, legal, or financial advice, and it should not be used as such.

Passages touching on legal proceedings are recorded by the name and date of the document, and are not a summary or an interpretation of any ruling.

The writer welcomes any correction accompanied by documentation. Documented corrections accepted by the publisher will be considered for later printings.

PART ONE

Red Earth

1971–1990 · Chapters 1–4

A road runs one hundred fifty-one kilometers from the sea to the highlands. In 1979 a family carried a child along it, away from Ngoc Diem and into a province that grew coffee.

Nothing in this part is about coffee as a business. It is about a place, a plant that is not native to it, quintals of paddy sold to pay for a seat in a lecture hall, and a plane ticket bought by an uncle to send a young man back to school.

CHAPTER 1

One Hundred Fifty-One Kilometers

From the Sea to the Highlands

There is a road about one hundred fifty-one kilometers long that joins the sea to the highlands.

It begins at Ninh Hoa, in Khanh Hoa province, runs west, climbs the Phoenix Pass, crosses into M'Drak district, and continues on to Buon Ma Thuot. Today a person drives it in a morning, stops for lunch in Buon Ma Thuot, and is still back in time.

In 1979 it was not like that.

Dang Le Nguyen Vu's family went up to M'Drak at a time when that road still carried people from one world into another.

He was born on February 10, 1971, at Ninh Hoa, in Khanh Hoa province.

The published sources stop at the two words Ninh Hoa. In Ninh Hoa itself the birthplace is named more exactly: Ngoc Diem hamlet, Ninh Ich commune, in the southern part of Ninh Hoa, about thirty-five kilometers north of Nha Trang. That is what the recorder was told on the ground, by people living there, and it is set down here as that and nothing more.

Ninh Ich commune no longer carries that name. On July 1, 2025, it was merged with Ninh Loc, Ninh Hung, and Ninh Tan to form the commune of Nam Ninh Hoa.

That country sits close to the sea and lives on salt flats, rice fields, and old craft villages strung along the highway. Coffee is not a plant of that place, and Khanh Hoa has never been a coffee province.

About thirty kilometers west of Ninh Hoa the road begins to lift. That lift is the Phoenix Pass, twelve kilometers of it, inside M'Drak district against the

Khanh Hoa line. Vehicles work up one bend at a time, engines straining, and everyone aboard knows they are climbing.

Past the pass the sea is gone from sight. The air is colder, the earth along the roadside changes color, and the familiar salt goes out of the wind.

Past the pass there is still some distance before M'Drak proper.

Where that family stopped is worth a remark.

Dak Lak is Vietnam's coffee capital, but not every part of the province is alike. The thickest belt of red basalt lies farther west, around Buon Ma Thuot and Krong Pak. M'Drak is on the eastern rim, just behind the pass, well away from that belt. The family traveled into the coffee province and halted in the part of it that is not on the coffee belt.

They went up to find somewhere else to live.
In the years after the war, many families from the

central coastal provinces went up to the Central Highlands. The coastal plain was crowded, the fields few, the people many. On the plateau there was still land to farm, and the state was establishing new agricultural stations. People did not go up there to find coffee, and not yet to find a fortune. They went up to find somewhere else to live.

The plateau was not empty land. The Ede, the M'Nong, and the Jarai had lived there long before there were plantations, before there was a highway, before there was coffee. The newcomers came after.

The child in that family was seven or eight when they went up to M'Drak in 1979.

Of the years that followed, only one person has given an account, and that person is Mr. Vu himself. In many later interviews he has described a farming childhood: breaking corn, tending pigs, making bricks alongside his mother, walking kilometers to school.

A family living off a hill farm, with nothing spare, and

for years on end no better off.

One thing can be looked up, and it belongs beside the rest.

In the year that family went up to M'Drak, Vietnamese coffee was almost nothing. By 1975, both halves of the country together held some 13,000 hectares, producing about 6,000 tons. By 1980 the area was about 23,000 hectares. In 1986 the whole country had roughly 50,000 hectares and made 18,400 tons.

Twenty years later the figure passed 800,000 tons.

The boy walking to school in M'Drak was walking there in the years before those figures moved.

CHAPTER 2

Why Coffee is Here

A Plant That is Not Native

The earth around Buon Ma Thuot is red.

Not the pale red of clayey soil down on the plain, but a deep red, close to brick brown, fine enough that one rain turns a pair of sandals into two clods. In the dry season that red dust settles on leaves, on roofs, on the clothes of anyone walking by. The French called the region terre rouge, red earth, and they called it that because they had come there looking for something.

The soil was left by volcanoes. Basalt cooled and then weathered over millions of years into a deep, loose, well-drained layer. Add a few hundred meters of elevation and a clearly divided wet and dry season, and you have something close to a set of conditions laid out in advance for the coffee plant.

But coffee is not a plant of Vietnam.

It comes from Africa. Arabica from the Ethiopian highlands, robusta from the damp forests of Central and West Africa. Europeans carried both across the tropics during the colonial period, along with rubber, tea, and sugarcane.

Arabica reached Vietnam in 1857, brought by the French, and the first trees were planted in the north in small numbers. Robusta arrived much later, not until 1908 — and it was robusta, not arabica, that would make the Central Highlands.

Vietnam's coffee industry did not begin on the plateau either. The first growing areas were scattered through Ninh Binh, Thanh Hoa, Nghe An, and then Quang Tri.

By the 1937–1938 crop year the whole country had about 13,000 hectares, yielding some 1,500 tons a season.

The Central Highlands came late. But when the French saw the plateau, they recognized that what they were looking for lay directly under their feet.

In 1922 a French agricultural company established the CADA plantation in Dak Lak, about 2,000 hectares, planted with coffee, rubber, and tea. That plantation sat on the road linking Buon Ma Thuot with Ninh Hoa — the same road a family coming up from the sea would travel half a century later.

Good soil is still not enough. There has to be the right plant. This whole book turns on that point.

There are two principal coffees in the world, and they are not alike.

Arabica prefers altitude and cool weather, and it accounts for most of the premium market in Europe and the United States — the coffee that is tasted and scored like wine.

Robusta tolerates heat, survives lower down, and

yields more from the same ground. The bean is strong and bitter, with markedly more caffeine. Western markets have generally rated it below arabica, and through most of its commercial history it has traded lower, going into instant coffee or into blends to bring the cost down.

But robusta has one merit the market cannot score: the plant lives. And it lives well across a great deal of the Central Highlands.

That is one of the reasons Vietnam became, over time, a robusta country.

Then Vietnamese people made that coffee into something of their own. The phin filter is a descendant of the French drip method. Condensed milk was used because for decades fresh milk was both hard to get and hard to keep. And the bean grown here is heavy, roasted dark, giving a very concentrated liquid that suits both the filter and the tin of milk. The three met in a single glass, over ice, and became a way of drinking coffee that is neither European nor American.

Then the industry took off, and the takeoff came in stages.

Doi Moi in 1986 was a general change of policy, not an order to distribute land. The right of a household to decide for itself on its own plot came later: Resolution 10 in 1988 gave farming households autonomy, and the Land Law of 1993 established long-term land-use rights that could be transferred and mortgaged.

From then the coffee area in the Central Highlands grew very fast. In 1986 the country had roughly 50,000 hectares. By 2000 the figure was about 517,000 hectares, with production near 800,000 tons. In the 1999–2000 crop year Vietnam passed Colombia to become the world's second-largest exporter of green coffee after Brazil, and the largest producer of robusta.

But behind a glass of coffee is a larger story, and the man who grows coffee is not the man who sets its price.

The bean leaves the farm as green coffee: dried,

unroasted, bagged, hauled down to the port. The reference price for robusta is formed on the futures market in London, now ICE Futures Europe, and it moves daily with the harvests in Brazil, Vietnam, and Indonesia, with weather, with stocks, with speculative money.

Between that number and the grower stand the trader, the exporter, the roaster, the distributor, along with regional differentials, lot quality, exchange rates, and freight. At every stage the value of the bean changes again.

However the arithmetic runs, the root of that number is decided thousands of kilometers from the farm, by people who have never seen it.

By the early 2000s the paradox was in plain sight. Vietnam planted the trees, picked the cherries, dried the beans, filled the sacks, and shipped a great deal of it out. But the largest share of added value — roasting, blending, packaging, naming, advertising, selling to the person who drinks it — sat somewhere else.

A country can be a production power without being a brand power. Those are two different things.

The world coffee market also has its brutal seasons. When supply outruns demand, prices fall to their lowest in decades, and in the early 2000s many coffee-growing households in the Central Highlands took heavy losses. In places people cut the trees down. What had been an asset a few years earlier became a burden. During the same period, in Western cities, people were still walking into shops, ordering a cup, and paying a price that had not fallen with the price the grower received.

That gap is not a gap of geography. It is the gap between the person who makes the raw material and the person who keeps the final value of the product.

In Buon Ma Thuot, a young man was beginning to see that gap.

He was not a coffee farmer, and not yet a businessman. He was studying medicine. But coffee was everywhere around him — in the sacks stacked by the roadside, in the small shops, on the farms of the plateau, and in the lives of the people he had been watching since he was a child in M'Drak.

Then a question began to form. If Vietnam can grow coffee for the whole world, why can Vietnam not have a coffee brand of its own?

That question was not yet Trung Nguyen. But it was where it started.

The boy who took that road from Ninh Hoa up to M'Drak had grown. And the road began to run the other way: not from the sea to the highlands, but from the highlands out to the world.

CHAPTER 3

The Price of a Seat

Quintals of Paddy

He passed the entrance examination.

In the account published in Tuoi Tre, Mr. Vu himself described what followed: the family had to sell several quintals of paddy and a number of other things in the house so that he could go down to Buon Ma Thuot and enroll.

A quintal of paddy is one hundred kilograms of unhusked rice.

For a hill-farming family, the rice in the house is not simply something to sell. The rice is next year's food. It is harvested, dried, put into the bin, and milled a little at a time until the following crop. Selling several quintals means drawing down in advance a portion of the food already set aside for the months ahead, and knowing beforehand that the end of the season will come up short.

What "other things in the house" were, the account does not say. Only that in a farm house in M'Drak at the end of the 1980s, the list of things that could be sold would not have been long.

The school at the end of that road was Tay Nguyen University, then inside the town of Buon Ma Thuot.

The university was established on November 11, 1977, under Decision 298-CP of the Government Council, charged with training university-level personnel for the development of the whole Central Highlands region. From the first day it had a Faculty of Medicine.

That detail is worth stopping on. A plateau that size, and the doctors for it were trained in one faculty, of one school, in one town. A student in M'Drak who wanted to study medicine and remain in the region had to come to Buon Ma Thuot.

The gate was narrow. And he got through it.
The medical program ran six years.

That figure makes the quintals of paddy look different. The rice sold was not paying for one year of study. It was the first installment on a six-year commitment, made by a family with nothing put by. In the years to come more money would have to be sent down, and at home there would still be only the farm.

What it bought was very concrete.

A son who becomes a doctor has a monthly salary, a position, and the means to hold up an entire household. In a mountain district a medical degree is not merely a matter of schooling or of pride. That degree is a way up.

The student who went down to Buon Ma Thuot carried a debt that was not written on paper.
He did not become a doctor.

CHAPTER 4

The Medical Lecture Hall

One Plane Ticket

Buon Ma Thuot in the early 1990s was still a town. Not until January 21, 1995, was it raised to a city.

The student from M'Drak studied and worked at the same time. Each time he went home and returned to school, his mother had to scrape together one or two hundred thousand dong for his fare.

In his account many years later, Mr. Vu remembers the years at the medical school as anything but settled study. The further he went, the more he turned over in his mind the work and the life of a physician.

What troubled him was specific.

He watched the classes ahead of him graduate. A civil servant's salary, as he saw it then, covered breakfast. To add lunch and dinner, to buy a house or a vehicle, most people trained in medicine would have to do things he considered hard to reconcile with the Hippocratic oath.

The conclusion he drew for himself was equally blunt: the surest way not to break that oath is not to take it. "And for me, the best way not to break the oath was to quit altogether and do something else."

In his third year, he decided to leave.

His mother wept until she had almost no tears left. Many of his classmates said he was not right in the head. By his account, only three friends in the class understood what he was thinking, and what he was thinking he put into a single line: he would not accept "sleeping in a narrow bed and dreaming small dreams."

Whether those three were the same friends who appear later in this story is not established by any source.

His friends emptied their pockets and gathered nearly a hundred thousand dong for him. With that, he caught a bus to Saigon, carrying the name and address of an uncle he had never met.

The uncle heard him out, then told him to go back to Dak Lak and finish his degree first. He promised that if his nephew still wanted to come to Saigon and go into business later, he would help. The plane ticket for the journey back was bought by the uncle as well.

The student was back at school a few days later.
A bus ticket carried him to Saigon. A plane ticket carried him back to Buon Ma Thuot.

That trip changed nothing on paper. He was still a medical student. But from then on he sat in the lecture hall with his head already somewhere else.

While studying, he began to look into coffee.

In his own account, it was during those years at the medical school that he began to investigate and research coffee. The friends in the rented room, the questions about the growers, about Vietnam exporting only raw beans, about processing, and then the trip to Tuy Hoa — all of it falls inside that stretch of time.

That is where everything begins.

But one thing remains unclosed to this day: the year he first sat in that lecture hall.

In the account published in Tuoi Tre in 2004, Mr. Vu himself says he passed the entrance examination for Tay Nguyen Medical School in 1990. Many later articles give 1992; VietnamNet, for instance, records him entering the Faculty of Medicine at Tay Nguyen University in 1992. And there is a third way of arriving at a date: he was born on February 10, 1971, so if a source says he entered university at twenty, that window runs from early 1991 into early 1992.

Two recorded years, and a third date derived from

his age. So far, no school record has been produced to close the matter.

The difference is not a biographer's trifle, because behind each figure is a quite different stretch of time.

If he enrolled in 1990, his third year falls in the 1992–93 or 1993–94 academic year, and from there to the first business licence of August 1996 there are three years or more. If he enrolled in 1992, his third year falls in 1994–95 or 1995–96, and the same stretch is little more than a year.

And a great deal happens inside that gap: a hand-cranked roaster, a trip to Tuy Hoa, a failure in Long Xuyen, a return, and finally a name.

No one has yet fixed a year to all of it. What can be measured at this point is not the date of each event, but the amount of room available for them.

More than one chronology remains possible. And the two produce two different working lives: a man who fumbled and failed repeatedly over several years before he could raise a name, and a man who did nearly all of it in a little over a year.

This book has not chosen a figure.

The Central Highlands then were opening new farms every year, with the harvest rising every season, and still the largest share of the bean's value lay elsewhere.

From an opening visible in the middle of a growing market, the story turns to the first people who tried, with him, to do what at the time had almost no model to follow: to roast, to brew, to sell, and to put a name on Vietnamese coffee.

PART TWO

The Roasting Drum

1990–1996 · Chapters 5–8

Four questions, asked by someone who stood outside the trade and therefore had time to ask them. A roasting formula given away in one afternoon by a woman whose name no source records. One drum turned by hand over a wood fire. A few kilos of green coffee taken on credit and paid for on the day promised.

Everything in this part is small enough to be repeated by anyone, in any trade, in any year. That is why it is here.

CHAPTER 5

Four Questions

What Was Not Yet Being Asked

The years the student spent in Buon Ma Thuot were also the years coffee in the Central Highlands began to take off.

The figures show it more plainly than any account. In 1994 alone, output rose 48.5 percent over the year before; in 1995 it rose 45.8 percent; in 1996 it added another 33 percent.

In a town that lives on coffee, numbers like those are not on paper. They are out in the street: new plots cleared, new houses going up, trucks queued to take on loads. The price of coffee becomes the daily conversation — the man holding stock works out whether to sell or hold, the man who borrowed to open a plot works out a whole season at a falling price.

The medical student lived in the middle of that, and began looking into coffee while he was still at school.

What he noticed was not whether the price was up or down. What he noticed was the thing that was not there.

The whole region made coffee, and the whole region sold it as green beans. The beans were dried, bagged, hauled to the port, and from the port went out into the world under the name of whoever bought them. In the shops in Buon Ma Thuot people drank good coffee, brewed in a phin, roasted on the premises, and belonging to no name at all.

Beyond the border, people knew Vietnamese coffee as a commodity, and did not yet know a Vietnamese coffee brand.

In Mr. Vu's later account, the question he was asking came to essentially this: why did a country that sold so much coffee have no coffee name of its own that anyone remembered?

Out of that question, later articles arranged four.

Why are coffee growers still poor? Why do countries that cannot grow the plant get rich from coffee? Why does Vietnam sell only raw beans? Why does it not process and name its own?

The four are tidy and well balanced. That tidiness is itself a reason for caution. What every source records in the same way is only the core: as a student, he was already asking why Vietnamese coffee went out into the world while a Vietnamese brand did not.

The question is not a difficult one. Anyone living in Buon Ma Thuot in those years had the facts in hand to ask it.

But it was not a question the trade was arranged to ask, and there was a practical reason.

The grower had a more urgent question: what is the price this week, sell or hold. The trader asked how many tons and what moisture content. The state enterprise asked about its export quota. Everyone in the chain had his own work, and every one of those jobs was heavy enough.

Putting a name on a commodity, making a stranger in another country remember that name and then pay more because of it — that belongs to a different trade. In Buon Ma Thuot at the time, that trade did not exist: no school in the region taught it, no one in the region had built a brand that traveled, and there was no model nearby to look at.

A student at the medical school asking the question had no advantage either. He knew nothing about brands, had no capital, no connections, and was studying an unrelated field. Nor did he stand outside the coffee chain. His family lived off a hill farm like most families around them.

What he did not have was a position in that chain.

No harvest of his own to sell. No note falling due. No shipment to deliver.

From where he stood, the gap was visible.

From seeing it to doing anything about it was a long way. The first thing he did was not write a plan. The first thing was to go and find someone who knew how to roast.

CHAPTER 6

The Night Bus

A Trade Secret, Given Away

A dried coffee bean is not yet coffee.

The bean is grey-green, hard, and nearly without smell. To become something drinkable it has to be roasted. In the drum it heats, loses water, swells, cracks, and turns from yellow to brown to dark brown. Sugars and amino acids in the bean meet under heat and produce hundreds of compounds that were not there in the raw seed.

Most of the bean's characteristic flavor is made in those ten or fifteen minutes. Under-roasted, it is sour and thin; over-roasted, the burn takes over everything. From the same batch of beans, two people roasting can produce two different drinks.

In Vietnam, some traditional roasting methods add another layer. The roaster puts in butter to make the beans glossy and to lift the aroma, a little salt, a little caramelized sugar for body and color, each house with its own proportions.

That formula is the property of the shop.

Nobody writes it down. Nobody teaches it. And nobody gives it away.

Here the student was no longer alone. By Mr. Vu's account there were four of them at the time, himself and the friends he shared a rented room with. They pooled their money and bought a roaster.

What they did not have was a way to use it.

There was a well-known coffee house in Tuy Hoa, and among their friends was someone with a connection there. Tuy Hoa sits on the coast of Phu Yen, east of the range that the road from Buon Ma Thuot has to cross on the way down to the plain.

On a day off, they took a bus.

They explained to the owner who they were and what they wanted. She listened, was moved by it, and passed on to them how she roasted and ground.

That is the whole of it. No account mentions a sum of money. No account mentions an agreement. A woman in the trade handed four strangers the very thing that made her own shop worth something.

That night they went back to Buon Ma Thuot on the late bus, back up the pass they had come down that morning.

What they carried home that night was more than equipment. It was a formula given away for nothing, by a woman whose name no source has yet recorded.

Her name does not appear in the writing that survives. There is no address for the shop, no identifying detail sufficient to trace her. In everything written about Trung Nguyen across thirty years, she appears exactly once, in a few lines, and then is gone.

Back from Tuy Hoa, they had the formula in hand.

But a formula does not make a coffee company.

CHAPTER 7

Cranked by Hand, Fired with Wood

The Neighbors Were Not Wrong

In Tuy Hoa they were given a formula. The formula assumed that whoever held it knew how to hold a fire.

The roaster they had pooled their money for was the hand-cranked drum type: a metal cylinder lying horizontal, a crank at one end, set over a wood fire. Pour in the beans, close the hatch, and turn. Turn evenly, turn without stopping, turn until the batch is done. Stop for half a minute and the beans against the wall of the drum scorch before the beans in the middle.

There was no thermometer on the drum. No timing chart. The roaster knows where a batch is by three things: sound, smell, and color. The first crack comes as a dry, scattered snapping. A few minutes later comes the second, denser and brittler. What happens between those two cracks decides what the cup will be, and the margin is under a minute wide.

Firewood obeys nobody. A wood flame rises and falls with the stick just laid on, with the draft through the door, with whether the wood is dry or still damp. The roaster has to make up for all of that with the crank and by moving the drum nearer the fire or further from it. Every batch is a guess, and the answer only appears after the beans are tipped out onto the screen.

A bad batch cannot be corrected. A ruined roast is a quantity of beans already paid for, thrown away.

The additives used in that style of roasting made the work harder by another degree. Caramelized sugar burns before the beans do at high heat. Butter melts and coats the wall of the drum, leaving a residue, and that residue joins the next batch. The drum has to be scraped.

Scraped badly, today's batch carries the taste of

yesterday's.

As the drum turns, the beans shed a papery skin called chaff, light enough to lift and settle in hair, on clothing, on every flat surface in the room.

And the smoke.

Roasting coffee makes smoke from the first minute and more of it every minute after. It is not like cooking smoke. It is thick, sweet, it clings, and it travels. A few kilos roasted in the back yard of a rented block is known to the whole block.

The roasting tended to fall in the evening, because the days were spent in the lecture hall.

A person next door has no answer to a smell. One house is drying laundry. Another has someone ill in it. Someone comes off a night shift needing sleep, and over the fence a few students are cranking a drum over a wood fire.

In every retelling of that period, the neighbors appear only as an obstacle. Read carefully, they were not wrong about anything. They were not standing in the way of a career; they were complaining about smoke in their own yard, at an hour when it should have been quiet.

The group kept roasting.

How many batches they went through before they had something sellable is recorded nowhere. What can be read out of what remains is that the stretch was long enough for them to learn how fast their own drum heated, which wood burned evenly, and how to hear the first crack and count the minutes left.

The formula was something received in one afternoon. The use of the formula had to be paid for one ruined batch at a time.

CHAPTER 8

Working Capital for People with No Capital

A Few Kilos at a Time

With the formula and the drum, the trouble moved elsewhere.

To sell roasted and ground coffee you first need green coffee to roast, and green coffee has to be bought. Buying means paying at once, while the money from selling comes in days later, sometimes weeks later.

The gap between paying for the beans and collecting from the buyer is working capital. Every trading business lives or dies in that gap, and the slower the goods sell, the wider it opens.

A man with a good product and no working capital sells nothing.

That group of students had none.

A bank was out: no collateral, no books, nothing to show but a few student cards. Family was out; their families had none either. The money they had pooled for the drum had been the last of it.

What they did was what people without money do.

They went to the green coffee dealers and asked to take the goods first and pay afterward, a few kilos each time. They carried it back, roasted, ground, packed it, and split up to bicycle it around to the shops in the area. When it sold, they collected, paid the dealer, and took the next lot.

It looks small. It was a mechanism.

What they lacked was money. What they used in place of money was trust.

The dealer who handed over the beans was not doing it out of pity. To a dealer, a few kilos is a cheap test:

lose it and you lose little, win and you have a standing customer. And precisely because the debt was small, the debt could be paid. Pay once and the next time you can ask for a little more.

Money was scarce. Credit was available only to someone who paid. In that small trade, reliability became a form of working capital.

The price of working that way was time and physical labor.

Taking small quantities meant the margin on each turn barely covered food. Increasing it meant more turns, and every turn covered the same ground: to the dealer for the beans, home to roast, grind, and pack, out to each shop to deliver, then back to each shop to collect.

Anyone can do it. But it has to be done a great many times. And they were still going to school.

This is the point at which the story is usually told half a beat wrong.

People tend to tell this stretch as a season of pitiable hardship, laid down as backing for the glory that follows. But read as a businessman would read it, this is not the pitiable part.

The later part of this story cannot be repeated by anyone. Taking delivery of a few kilos and paying on the day you said you would — anyone can do that, in any trade, in any year.

It went on like that for some time.

Then came the point at which what they were selling needed a name.

PART THREE

When the Name Begins

1996–2003 · Chapters 9–15

Two hundred million dong borrowed from a family nobody can name. A business with two birthdays sixty days apart. A defeat in Long Xuyen and the road back. Friends whose names appear on an application and then leave the file.

Then an address in Phu Nhuan, ten days of free coffee, a first border crossed, and a hall in Saigon where the labels were taken off the cups.

CHAPTER 9

Two Hundred Million

The Bicycle, and the Borrowed Money

There are two accounts of Trung Nguyen's founding capital, and both come from people who were there.

The brand's official site says that when Trung Nguyen came into being in 1996, its first capital asset was an old bicycle, together with the faith and will of youth.

At the hearing of February 20, 2019, more than twenty years after the start, in argument over who had built the business, Mr. Dang Le Nguyen Vu said that when he began he had borrowed two hundred million dong from a family. He also said that for twenty-three years afterward he had sent that family twenty-five million dong a month in acknowledgment of the debt.

Two hundred million dong in 1996 was not a small sum. Measured against domestic gold prices recorded for that year, it came to dozens of taels.

Set side by side, the two accounts do not necessarily contradict each other. One speaks of the first tangible asset; the other of the money used to begin trading.

The bicycle is transport. A bicycle can carry coffee out to the shops; it cannot buy coffee to roast.

A sum like two hundred million is another matter. That money creates the ability to buy stock, to pay for raw material, and to open a cycle of capital that a bicycle cannot open. It is precisely what the deliveries of a few kilos were short of: working capital.

With a group turning over a few kilos at a time, a sum like that, if it was in fact in hand, would be enough to change how they bought — buying outright instead of asking for credit, buying more each time, no longer having to collect from one shop before they could take delivery for another.

On the repayment, the testimony is one thing and other people's arithmetic is another.

What Mr. Vu said in court was three figures: two hundred million, twenty-five million a month, twenty-three years. The figure of 6.9 billion that appeared in the press afterward is the newspaper's own multiplication, not his words. And the further statement that he repaid nearly thirty-five times what he borrowed is a division laid on top of that multiplication.

The division does not mean much. Two hundred million in 1996 and payments of twenty-five million spread out to 2019 do not have the same purchasing power, so adding them up and dividing by the original loan compares two things that cannot be compared.

What is worth recording is not the ratio.

What is worth recording is that a family put a very large sum, for that time, behind a young man at the start of his working life. And that the young man repaid it across twenty-three years, including years in which twenty-five million a month had become very small against what he had.

In the accounts that survive, that family has no name. Where they lived, what they did, how they knew Mr. Vu, and why they trusted him are all unrecorded. They occupy the same position as the woman with the shop in Tuy Hoa: present at a decisive turn, then gone from the story.

They had coffee to sell.
What was missing was a name.

CHAPTER 10

A Business with More Than One Birthday

June 16, or August 15

Trung Nguyen has two dates of origin, exactly two months apart, and both fall in 1996.

The brand's official site gives June 16, 1996, as the day Dang Le Nguyen Vu founded Trung Nguyen in Buon Ma Thuot. That is the date by which the brand counts its own age, and in 2026 the thirtieth-anniversary observance was set on it as well.

According to the business registration records quoted in the press, the first licence was issued by the People's Committee of Buon Ma Thuot on August 15, 1996, in the name of Mr. Dang Le Nguyen Vu.

Two dates, two ways of counting. Both can be correct

within what each is describing.

A trading concern has several ways of reckoning its age: the day work began, the day the sign went up, the day the state issued a licence, the day a legal person came into existence. Those four rarely coincide.

Here one further point has to be made plain, because it changes what the figure of thirty years means.

What was licensed on August 15, 1996, according to the sources quoted, was a household business registered to one individual. A household business is not a legal person, and the individual named is liable for the business with his own property.

The organization bearing the name Trung Nguyen changed legal form several times afterward. According to documents quoted in the press, on July 19, 1999, the Trung Nguyen Coffee Enterprise Cooperative was established. According to the file cited by counsel at the 2019 hearing, on December 2, 2002, the cooperative became Trung Nguyen Coffee Company

Limited, with charter capital of 16 billion dong. Then on April 12, 2006, Trung Nguyen Joint Stock Company came into being, later named Trung Nguyen Group Joint Stock Company.
So how old Trung Nguyen is depends on the question.

If the question is when the name appeared on the market, the answer is 1996. If it is when an organization with its own legal standing bearing the name Trung Nguyen appeared, the answer is 1999. If it is when there was a company in the present sense, the answer is 2002, or 2006.

What is notable is not that the figures disagree. What is notable is the date the brand chose for itself.

June 16 comes before the licence date in the record as quoted. That is, in counting its own age, Trung Nguyen does not count from the state's piece of paper. It counts from the day the founders started work.

A business choosing its birthday is also choosing a story about itself.

And the licence of August 15 holds something the official site does not. According to counsel's presentation at the 2019 hearing, the business application carried the name of Mr. Dang Le Nguyen Vu together with four friends, all of them students.

But here a different number appears. The accounts told for years describe a group of four, that is, Mr. Vu and three friends. The file cited by counsel in court shows five.

The book has not chosen between them.

In everything published about Trung Nguyen, that is one of very few traces of those friends on paper.

CHAPTER 11

Two Defeats, and the Road Back to Saigon

Long Xuyen

With a name, and with stock, the next step was to go further than Buon Ma Thuot.

Saigon was the first place they aimed at.

What happened on that attempt the accounts barely preserve. Only that Trung Nguyen moved on Saigon and failed quickly, not being strong enough to compete in a market where the coffee sellers were already many and already long established. No dates, no address, no figures.

After that, they turned in another direction.

The Mekong Delta was then a large market that few

roasters paid attention to. Long Xuyen was chosen as the stopping point. There the group found a partner, and the two sides opened a roasting operation together.

The partnership went nowhere. By Mr. Vu's account, the two sides differed deeply on outlook and on how to do business: the other man looked to the gain in front of him, while he wanted to build a brand. Within a few months, the partnership broke.

Something that sounds like a personal falling-out was enough to bring down an entire operation.

In a small business, two people who go in together usually have nothing between them but a promise.

There are no articles setting out who decides what. There is no reserve of capital to carry a losing season. There is nobody to arbitrate when the two think differently. In practice every decision needs both men to nod, so two men looking in two directions is enough to stop the business where it stands.

By Mr. Vu's account, he lost everything he had put in.

What came back from Long Xuyen was a few items still usable: glasses, cups, filters, spoons. A very compact way of saying that the plan had failed.

The lesson he drew from it he also stated compactly: in going into business with someone, you must agree on outlook and on method, and above all you must choose the right person to work with.

The sentence sounds self-evident. But the man saying it had paid everything he owned to learn it, and that is the distance between a maxim and a lesson.

One more fragment survives from this stretch of road. The original interview behind it cannot be traced, so it is recorded here strictly as an account and nothing more: on the way back to Saigon, the old Honda Dame carrying him broke in two, and that night the group slept in Bach Tung Diep park in District One.

There is something worth noting about the places.

Saigon is where Trung Nguyen lost the first time. Long Xuyen is where Trung Nguyen lost everything. And from Long Xuyen the road back did not lead up to Buon Ma Thuot. It led back to Saigon.

This time he stayed.

CHAPTER 12

The People Without Names

A Disappearance with Paperwork

Three sets of people enter this story at decisive turns, and then nobody knows where they went.

The first is the woman with the shop in Tuy Hoa. She gave away, for nothing, the thing that made her own shop worth something, to four strangers, in one afternoon.

The second is the family that lent two hundred million at a time when the borrower had nothing to offer but a promise.

The third is the friends.

Of the first two, this is all the book can record. No

names, no addresses, no identifying detail sufficient to follow.

The third set is different. They left a trace, and the trace has a date at either end.

According to counsel's presentation at the 2019 hearing, the 1996 business application carried the name of Mr. Dang Le Nguyen Vu together with four friends, all students. That is the occasion on which they exist on paper.

Then at the registration of change dated November 27, 2000, the list of management members added one person: Mr. Dang Mo, born 1946, Mr. Vu's father.

On that list no student friend appears any longer.

Four years between two pieces of paper. They signed when there was nothing, and left before there was everything. The person remaining beside the man who filed the application was that man's own father.

What happened between those two dates no document says. One account holds that after repeated failures the friends withdrew one by one, some returning to medicine, some going another way. That account is plausible, and it remains an account.

Even the number is unclosed. Mr. Vu's own words and a number of press articles give a group of four, that is, himself and three friends from the rented room. The file cited by counsel gives five.

As for their names, no source has published them, and this book has not gone looking. Those people left the story twenty-five years ago, and they are under no obligation to return to it because somebody else's story wants more detail.

In a book about a large business, readers usually want to know who founded it, and the answer usually consists of a single name. But no business is ever built by a name.

Some people put in money. Some put in work. Some

were simply present at the hardest point, when nobody yet knew where any of it was going.

That is the easiest thing to forget when looking back from now. The reader today knows the ending, and so it is easy to imagine that the people at the beginning knew it too. They did not. In that year, nobody knew how long the name Trung Nguyen would last.

The people without names are present in the part of the story before there was any light, and they left before the light began.

CHAPTER 13

Ten Free Days, in a City That Already Drank Coffee

587 Nguyen Kiem

A house number on Nguyen Kiem Street, Phu Nhuan district. Not a central street, not expensive frontage, not a place anyone walks past and remembers.

In August 1998, Trung Nguyen opened its first coffee shop in Saigon there.

Saigon had been drinking coffee for a very long time. People knew the phin, knew iced black, knew condensed milk, knew the small shops with chairs put out on the pavement. Coffee was not something that needed introducing.

So the problem facing a name from Buon Ma

Thuot walking into Saigon was not to make people understand what coffee was. The problem answered a harder question: why should they drink this coffee, when the shop they already go to is still there and still opens every day.

The answer Trung Nguyen chose was very simple.

For the first ten days, the coffee was free. Anyone walking past could come in and drink.

It was not a complicated campaign, and it did not need to be. A brand nobody has heard of cannot tell people it is good, because there is nothing behind the claim. But a cup of coffee set down in front of someone speaks for itself.

Giving it away moves the burden of proof from the words to the product.

The test is also blunt with the seller. If the customer likes it, he comes back and pays for the next one. If he does not, the seller knows at once where he stands, and knowing early is better than knowing late.

The cost is plain. Ten days of free coffee is ten days of raw material gone, ten days of rent, ten days of wages for whoever brewed it, and no revenue at all. For a business that had lost all its capital in Long Xuyen not long before, ten days was not a light decision.

That is the part worth noting. Not the cleverness of the idea, but the placing of nearly everything that remained on an outcome that depended on whether strangers came back.

Of what happened during those ten days the record preserves very little. How many came on the first day, whether the fifth was busy or empty, how many became regulars, what the takings were afterward — none of it was kept, and none of it should be invented to make the story better.

What is known is that the shop held, and that other shops came after it.

In 2000, Trung Nguyen went to Hanoi. In 2001, the brand crossed a border for the first time.

But before all of those steps there was an address on Nguyen Kiem Street, and ten days in which anyone walking past could come in and drink for nothing.

CHAPTER 14

Crossing a Border for the First Time

Khoi Nguon Sang Tao

A coffee shop needs an address. A brand that means to travel needs more than that.

In 2001, Trung Nguyen franchised in Japan and Singapore.

At home the brand still had something to stand on. Vietnamese people were used to dark-roasted coffee, used to the phin, used to that way of drinking, and had been for a long time. Outside the border those supports were gone.

In Japan people drink coffee in another way, in shops with traditions of their own, to a taste that dark-roasted robusta does not already sit inside. In

Singapore the market was small but open, and anyone could walk into it.

The choice of franchising had a practical reason too. A five-year-old business does not have the money or the people to open its own outlets abroad. Franchising lets someone on the ground put up the capital and run the place, while the brand contributes the name, the formula, and the method.

But franchising demands something that selling coffee does not: the model has to be repeatable. A shop that is good because the owner has the touch cannot be copied. To copy it, there has to be something that can be written down, taught, and made to produce the same result in a place where you are not present.

In the same year, by the company's own list of milestones, Trung Nguyen announced the slogan that would stay with the brand for a long time: Khoi nguon sang tao, rendered in the company's English-language materials as Explore creative inspiration. That list places the slogan and the Japan and Singapore franchising in a single entry for 2001. It gives no day and no month.

The line is notable for where it puts its weight.

A coffee brand can talk about the bean, the growing region, the roast, the flavor. Khoi nguon sang tao does not talk about the cup. It talks about the person drinking, and about what happens after the drinking.

That is a calculated choice. To speak of flavor is to compete on flavor, and in a contest of taste a young robusta brand does not easily beat names that have been there a hundred years. To speak of creativity is to change the field.

The word did not remain a slogan. In time it became a product name as well, and the two should not be run together. Khoi nguon sang tao is what the brand says about itself. Ca phe Sang tao is a range of roast-and-ground blends sold in numbered boxes.

The range runs from Sang tao 1 to Sang tao 5, with

a separate Sang tao 8 placed above them, and the numbers mark what is in the bag rather than a scale of strength: number 1 from culi robusta; number 2 a robusta and arabica blend; number 3 from arabica grown around Buon Ma Thuot; number 4 a blend of arabica, robusta, excelsa, and catimor; number 5 from culi arabica. Number 8, blended from arabica and robusta, is sold as the top of the range, and the company's own copy attaches it to heads of state and to diplomacy.

On packaging sold outside Vietnam the range is printed in English as Creative: Creative 1 through Creative 5, and Creative 8.

When the range first appeared, the sources consulted here do not say. What can be said is that it came after the slogan, and that the device it uses — a ladder of numbers a customer can climb — is the same device that would be explained across a counter in Westminster, California, in 2023.

Of what actually took place in those two markets —

how many outlets, who the partners were, what the contracts said, what came of it — the available record is not enough to tell. Only what has been confirmed is kept: in 2001, Trung Nguyen franchised in Japan and Singapore.

What matters is not the scale. In 2001 Trung Nguyen was not large, and those two markets were not the world.

What matters is that before that year a border was a line on a map. After it, a border was something that could be crossed.

CHAPTER 15

A Test That Withheld the Names

G7

On November 23, 2003, at the Reunification Palace, Trung Nguyen introduced a new product and a way of introducing a product that the Vietnamese market had not seen before.

The product was instant coffee, called G7.

The method of introduction was a blind tasting.

Participants were handed two cups of instant coffee, unlabeled, unnamed, without packaging. Drink, then choose the one you prefer. Only after choosing were you told whose you had picked.

The whole force of that method lies in removing the

thing the other side had more of: the name.

On a shelf, a long-established international brand carries everything it has accumulated — years of advertising, familiar packaging, the safety of the thing you already use. A new Vietnamese name has none of it. Compared on the shelf, there is no comparison.

Take the labels away and both sides are left with exactly one thing: the liquid in the cup.

The figure Trung Nguyen announced after the test was that 89 percent of participants chose G7, with about eleven thousand people taking part.

That figure should be read at its proper size. It is a number announced by the company about a test the company organized. The result says what happened that day, at that place, among the people who were there. To say that Vietnamese consumers in general preferred G7 goes further than a tasting can prove.

But set the figure aside and the method is still worth

remembering, because the method says something very direct: we do not yet have the standing you have, so we propose leaving standing out of the contest.

And there is something G7 changed inside Trung Nguyen's own business, no less important.

Until then, drinking Trung Nguyen coffee meant going to a Trung Nguyen shop. The name stayed in one place and waited for people to come to it.

A packet of instant coffee waits for nobody. A packet of G7 could go into a household kitchen, into an office drawer, into the suitcase of someone traveling, onto the shelf of a grocery in a province the brand had never set foot in.

From then on, G7 coffee did not need a door to open. G7 needed a shelf to sit on.

Whose shelf it was is the business of the years that followed.

PART FOUR

The Ecosystem

2004–2022 · Chapters 16–22

The name leaves the shop it was poured in and goes onto somebody else's shelf. A title arrives that nobody conferred. Books are given away. Companies multiply around a single name. Horses appear on the hills of Krong A.

Four dates are recorded here for the years that are not written at length, and nothing more is said about them.

CHAPTER 16

Nine Thousand Five Hundred Points of Sale

Somebody Else's Shelf

A packet of coffee sitting on the shelf of a grocery has traveled a long way.

The bean was picked on some plot in the Central Highlands, dried, ground, roasted, packed, hauled, and finally brought to rest at the eye level of a person doing the shopping. That person stands in front of the shelf for a few seconds. Reaches out, or does not.

That is where everything is decided.
But the shelf does not belong to the person who made the coffee.

The shelf belongs to the shopkeeper. The shopkeeper decides what goes at eye level, what sits down by the floor, and what is not reordered because it moved slowly last month. However good a roaster is, once his goods leave his own store they are one name among many on a shelf he does not own.

In 2003, G7 came out and put Trung Nguyen onto those shelves.

Three years later, Trung Nguyen took a further step: making the shelf itself.

The name of that step was G7 Mart.

In 2006, domestic reports recorded Trung Nguyen announcing the G7 Mart system with about five hundred stores, total investment of some 475 billion dong, and a target of building toward roughly nine thousand five hundred points of sale.

Set the three figures side by side and the shape of the plan is visible. Five hundred is what could be counted. Four hundred seventy-five billion is what had been spent to have something countable. Nine thousand five hundred is a horizon.

How wide the distance between those numbers was can be measured by going back eight years.

In 1998, at 587 Nguyen Kiem, Trung Nguyen opened its first coffee shop in Saigon, and gave the coffee away for the first ten days.

One shop, and a giveaway that lasted ten days.

Eight years later the question on the table was no longer how to get people to walk into your shop, but how to be present in nine thousand five hundred places people walk past every day.

If it worked, the buyer would no longer have to go looking for Trung Nguyen. He would step into a store near home and the name would already be on the shelf.

At this point the problem changes form entirely, and the change is worth stating plainly.
Opening a coffee shop is a matter of premises,

staff, supplies, and regulars. Running a network of thousands of points of sale is a different trade. Goods have to be held in which warehouse, moved by what vehicle, delivered to which store first and which second. The money locked up in stock spread across such a network is very large, and it has to be real money, not borrowed for the moment. Every additional store is one more place that can run out, sit unsold, or do something wrong that nobody at the center can see.

The number of stores rises in a line; the number of things to watch rises faster.

Nine thousand five hundred, then, was never only a figure about stores. It was a problem of organization.

One more thing has to be said directly.

Nine thousand five hundred was a target announced in 2006, not a count of points of sale in operation. The available record supports recording about five hundred stores announced alongside that target, and does not support turning a target into an achievement.

Distinguishing the two does not make the number smaller.

In 2006, counting from June 16, 1996, Trung Nguyen was exactly ten years old. Ten years earlier the story had been a hand-cranked drum, night buses, and a few kilos of coffee taken on credit. Ten years on, the story was hundreds of billions of dong in announced investment and a network of thousands of points of sale imagined.

In those ten years the company's question had changed from how to survive to how to cover a market.

There is no network of nine thousand five hundred G7 Marts across the country today as first imagined. But the figure keeps its value as a marker, because it says something very clear about the moment it was spoken.

In 2006, Trung Nguyen no longer wanted merely to be the seller of the best coffee.

Trung Nguyen wanted to be the builder of the road.

CHAPTER 17

A Title Nobody Conferred

The Coffee King

From about the middle of the 2000s, Dang Le Nguyen Vu came to be widely known as the coffee king. The phrase came from the press, from people watching the market, and was then repeated often enough to become part of his public face.

What is interesting is not the word king. It is the question: why was a man in coffee called that at all?

Go back to 1996 and the question sounds remote. A new name, a small operation, a market in which those who came before had solid positions. Nobody looking at a man standing beside a roasting drum would know that thirty years later the press would address him with a word reserved for monarchs. Titles usually arrive after the fact, not before it.

By the early 2000s the picture had begun to change. Trung Nguyen was no longer a coffee shop in Saigon. There was Hanoi, there were franchises in Japan and Singapore, there was G7, there was the blind tasting at the Reunification Palace, and then G7 Mart with its ambition to build a distribution network outright. With each of those steps, the man behind the brand was looked at differently: not merely a businessman, but a figure bound up with the story of Vietnamese coffee.

Here is something rarely said. The Vietnamese coffee industry at that time had export companies far larger than Trung Nguyen, measured in tons and in dollars. Nobody called their executives the coffee king. They sold green coffee, goods that go into sacks and onto ships, carrying nobody's name and having no face behind them. Trung Nguyen sold a name. And a name can be crowned; a sack of goods cannot.

The difference between claiming a title and being given one is also worth keeping. If a man calls himself king, the story is about personal ambition. When the phrase comes from outside, the story is about an image that has formed in other people's eyes. The two are not the same.

Even so, king is a very large word, and the kind of word that generates a glow. There was no throne. There was no mechanism that conferred the title, and no document recording that he held such a post. There was only a form of address that took shape outside, and a run of results that people outside could see: a large domestic brand, an instant coffee that sold, and a name that had gone beyond the border.

The title appeared just as Trung Nguyen was turning from a business that sold coffee into a brand that wanted to talk about more than coffee. Coffee began to be attached to creativity, to aspiration, to entrepreneurial spirit, to a way of looking at the country. Dang Le Nguyen Vu also began appearing in conversations wider than his own industry: about young people, about national ambition, about building a Vietnamese brand able to stand outside in the world.

Coffee king was therefore only the top layer. Beneath it was a man who wanted to be seen as more than a man who sold coffee.

And from there a circle began to turn. The larger the brand, the harder it becomes to separate the founder from it. His name attaches to the company's name, personal statements are read as company statements, and then the company's success comes back to enlarge the image of the founder. Trung Nguyen made Dang Le Nguyen Vu's reputation, and Dang Le Nguyen Vu became the largest part of how the public saw Trung Nguyen.

Later the brand would change what it called itself, Trung Nguyen Legend would appear, new concepts would be brought into the story. The image of the founder stayed where it was. Coffee king became the marker of a period, the period in which Trung Nguyen was seen first of all as the growth of a Vietnamese coffee brand, before the story moved into chapters with more legal persons in them, more figures, more assets.

The word did not stay with one company either. In October 2016 a coffee brand called King Coffee was launched in the United States by TNI Corporation, at a Vietnamese-language variety show, and brought back to Vietnam in August 2017. TNI's chief executive is Le Hoang Diep Thao, a co-founder of Trung Nguyen, whose name appears in the 2014 shareholder register recorded later in this book. Sources disagree on the year TNI itself was founded and on when she ceased running the group, and this book chooses neither.

So Vietnamese coffee has a man the press calls the coffee king, and a separate brand carrying the word king on the packet, owned by someone else. Press accounts have described the second name as an answer to the first. No document establishes that, and this book does not repeat it as fact.

A title given from outside can be very handsome. But once a man has been called king, the reader naturally wants to know one thing the title cannot answer: What was the kingdom built out of?

CHAPTER 18

When the Brand Began Talking About Something Other Than Coffee

Books Given Away

By 2012 the phrase coffee king had settled into the newspapers. Around the same time, Trung Nguyen pushed forward a program called the Journey of Great Ambition.

The content of the program was not coffee. It was books.

Not books on brewing, not books about growing regions, not product literature. Books about aspiration, about will, about how a young person looks at the road ahead. And the books were given away, not sold.

A printed book costs paper, labor, storage, and freight.

The recipient pays nothing, and there is no assurance that a single additional packet of coffee will be sold. Measured as a sales campaign, the method produces no figure at all.

Measured another way, it does.

An advertisement asks a few seconds of you. A book asks more than that: it has to be opened, a page read, then another. The gift stays in the house, on a desk, in a classroom bookcase, and the name printed on the half-title stays with it.

Before this, the company's question had been how to sell roasted and ground coffee, then how to get an instant packet onto a shelf beside international names. Here the question changes: what should the drinker be thinking when holding that cup.

The figure announced for the program was one hundred million copies.

That is the scale of a national program rather than

a marketing activity. The figure came from the company, attached to a plan running over years, and the number of books actually reaching readers in any given year is not set out in a table by any of the reports.

By 2013 the program was extended further, tied to G7's tenth anniversary.

Set beside the hand-cranked drum in the back yard of a rented block, the distance is long. On one side, a few students roasting a few kilos to deliver to shops around the district. On the other, a company printing books to give to people who may not drink its coffee, and speaking about the will of a whole generation.

A thin line runs through this place.

A brand that speaks about large values is easily remembered, and just as easily oversteps its part. The person receiving the book may read it and keep something from it, or may turn the cover, see the name of a coffee company, and ask who is speaking and in what capacity.

This book does not answer that question. Setting what a brand says beside what that brand has done is enough.

From here on, coffee was no longer the only thing bearing the name Trung Nguyen.

On October 26, 2025, at the Coffee City development in Buon Ma Thuot, Trung Nguyen Legend broke ground on a kindergarten and a primary school.

Two other education companies are named as the operators: INschool for the kindergarten, Xanh Tue Duc for the primary school.

According to the announcement, the kindergarten is two floors, twenty-six classrooms, planned for six hundred fifty pupils; the primary school is three floors, twenty classrooms, planned for five hundred.

Each holds a reading room called the Light Library, stocked with the Tu sach Nen tang Doi doi collection, the same books the company had been giving away since 2012.

The announcement states that both schools will take their first intake in the 2026–2027 school year.

As of September 2026 no report of an opening day has been found.

CHAPTER 19

The Horses on the Krong A Hills

Back to M'Drak

In 2009, while he had a large coffee project in mind, Dang Le Nguyen Vu bought a great many horses and brought them to his farm in Dak Lak.
Ten years later a journalist went up to visit and counted about fifty, Arabian stock, the second generation born on the place. The man who kept them said the herd would come at a call, but would bunch together the moment they caught sight of the owner; and that in earlier times he had gone up the hill every day, while lately it was much less often.

The farm lies in Krong A commune, M'Drak district, Dak Lak province, against the foot of the mountains. On its area every article gives a different figure, from six hundred to eight hundred hectares. What they agree on is that the scale is counted in hundreds of hectares of hill.

It is the same district a family moved to in 1979, bringing a child with them.

The 2019 report records a place built in the opposite direction from everything else in this book. No television. No wifi. No single-use plastic in the guest rooms: shower gel, shampoo, and toothpaste all in large refillable containers. The first building, called the House on the Hill, had been in use a little over a month when the journalist came. By the plan, the whole site would have at most five clusters of villas, three to five rooms each, holding eight to twelve guests. For the six months of rain each year it closes, receives nobody, and is maintained.

Guests there could ride, were guided in yoga and meditation, and ate what the farm produced. The owner's own quarters were not within the part set aside for guests. Before that visit, a group of architects and a Japanese Zen master had come up to survey the site for a Japanese-style meditation garden.

Set against the chapters before it, this place is a subtraction.

A company had spent twenty years getting its name into as many places as possible: nine thousand five hundred points of sale in the plan, one hundred million books in the promise, more than sixty countries on the packaging. And the same man built on a hill a place holding at most twelve guests, closed half the year, with no signal and no screens.

Not a place made to expand. A place designed to be small.

From about 2013 the press began describing M'Drak as where he spent most of his time, and his public appearances thinned out. That stretch ran for years.

No document explains why he chose this hill rather than another, and no explanation is required. This is the district where the vehicle carrying his family stopped in 1979, after the pass. Forty years later on the hills in that district there is a herd of Arabian horses born on the place, in its second generation.

CHAPTER 20

When One Name Becomes Many Companies

3160 Billion

The coffee drinker sees only one name.

The G7 packet says Trung Nguyen. The shop sign says Trung Nguyen. In the buyer's mind it is one company, with one owner, making coffee.

Behind that single name, by the end of the 2000s, there was already a group of companies. One held the factories, one handled franchising, one held the trading side. Then in 2009 another was formed with a task quite unlike the others: Trung Nguyen Investment Joint Stock Company, with charter capital recorded at 3,160 billion dong.

The figure is far larger than any that has appeared in

this story. Two hundred million borrowed in 1996. Four hundred seventy-five billion announced for G7 Mart in 2006. Then three thousand one hundred sixty billion.

But what matters is not the size. It is the word standing in front of it.

A coffee company buys beans, roasts, packs, and sells. An investment company does none of that. An investment company holds shares in other companies.

This is a point to pause on, because it decides the rest of the story.

While a business is small, the owner is the operator, and the assets are things you can touch: the drum, the vehicle, the stock, the cash in the drawer. Whoever holds the keys is the owner. When a business grows and divides into several legal persons, ownership leaves the things you can touch. The owner is no longer the man holding the keys to the factory, but the man holding shares in the legal person that holds the shares of that factory.

A structure like that has practical reasons. Separating legal persons separates risk, so that one loss-making line does not pull the whole system down. It makes raising money easier, since an investor can buy into one line rather than the entire group. And each line keeps its own books, which makes it easier to see where the profit is and where the loss.

The price attached is rarely mentioned at the time the companies are set up. In such a structure, the question of who owns the business can no longer be answered by looking at who is running it. The answer sits in shareholder registers, and those pieces of paper can say something different from what everyone sees day to day.

The figure of 3,160 billion also has to be read for what it is. Charter capital is a legal concept: the level of capital shareholders undertake to contribute under the law, recorded in the company file. It should not be read as though Trung Nguyen had 3,160 billion dong in cash to spend in 2009. It is a figure describing a structure, not a figure describing a safe. And because it describes a structure, it is worth noticing.

Looking back over the road, there is a sequence. In 1996, a name. In 2003, G7 turned the name into goods sold on other people's shelves.

In 2006, G7 Mart set out to make the shelf; and in the same year the joint-stock structure took form. Then three years later the word investment appeared in a company's name. Product, brand, system, capital.

Each step pulled the business further from the image of a roasting operation in Buon Ma Thuot, and made the story harder to see from outside.

Those papers lay untouched for years with nobody paying attention. According to the file cited by counsel at the 2019 hearing, by the twenty-second registration of change, dated June 10, 2014, the company's charter capital was 2,500 billion dong. Mr. Dang Le Nguyen Vu held 51 percent. Ms. Le Hoang Diep Thao held 28 percent. Mr. Dang Mo, Mr. Vu's father, held 10 percent. The remainder was divided between a company within the group and one further individual.

Those figures look dry, and they become important only when the people named on them are no longer looking in the same direction.

Through the same period, the visible part of Trung Nguyen went on rising. The factory in Binh Duong had been operating since 2005. By 2010 the products were recorded as present in more than sixty countries and territories. The people drinking the coffee in those places picked up the packet and still saw only one name.

But what happened next did not happen at a factory, and did not happen in a foreign market.

It happened on registration papers.

CHAPTER 21

The Years Not Written at Length

Four Dates

In 2015 a civil matter began. It ran for six years and passed through three levels of court.

On March 27, 2019, the first-instance judgment was issued. On December 5, 2019, the appellate judgment was issued. On March 11, 2021, cassation Decision No. 01/2021/HNGD-GDT was issued. On May 21, 2021, the payment obligation under the enforcement decision was completed.

Four dates, three documents, one enforcement decision. This chapter is short by rule, not by omission. That is the whole of what this chapter records.

Through the same period, the name Trung

Nguyen Legend appeared in the course of a brand repositioning. Two lines run in parallel across the same years, and this book keeps them apart.

In 2021 the name passed its twenty-fifth year from Buon Ma Thuot.

CHAPTER 22

Three Ways of Brewing, One Way of Seeing Coffee

Ottoman, Roman, Zen

There is a cup of coffee that leaves a trace of itself.

The grounds are milled very fine, finer than for a phin, then put straight into a small pot with water and brought to the boil. No filter basket, no filter paper, no perforated steel. Poured into the cup, the grounds come with it. Drink it down and a dark sediment remains at the bottom.

Someone used to the phin finds it strange. Someone used to espresso finds it strange too.

That is the brewing method Trung Nguyen calls Ottoman.

Beside Ottoman is Roman, and beside Roman is Zen. After a course of research into the history, culture, and economics of coffee, Trung Nguyen Legend views the world of coffee through three coffee civilizations: Ottoman, Roman, and Zen. That way of putting it needs to be set in its proper place.

This is not a classification used by coffee scholarship, nor a term already in the literature. It is a way of seeing devised by the company itself, and the company says as much each time it introduces it. The three names are not three varieties of bean, nor three product lines in the ordinary sense. The three names are a frame for looking.

The history behind the frame is real and already long. Coffee came out of the lands east of Africa, across the Arabian peninsula, into the Islamic world, and then spread along the trade routes. Each place that received it made its own way of drinking: a grind, a vessel, a ritual, a kind of room. The Vietnamese received coffee from the French and produced the phin and the habit of condensed milk. Everyone was doing the same thing

with a bean that came from somewhere else.
What Trung Nguyen did was gather those layers into three groups and give them names.

Ottoman, as the group describes it, is one of the cradles of world coffee civilization, where coffee was regarded as a drink of alertness and creative stimulation. The method that leaves sediment at the bottom of the cup takes time, and the drinker has to wait.

Roman, still by that description, stands for bringing science and engineering into production, for precision in preparation, for the art of presentation and appreciation. If Ottoman is the copper pot and the flame, Roman is the machine, the pressure, the number. The same bean, two entirely different roads.

Zen turns coffee inward. Slower, quieter, with fewer words. A cup becomes a pause, not necessarily saying anything further.

The point worth noting is here, and it is there in how the group presents itself. Ottoman existed already.

Roman existed already. Both belong to other lands and other centuries, and Trung Nguyen can only recount them. But speaking of the third civilization, the group speaks in a different voice — that with Zen coffee, Trung Nguyen has raised Vietnamese coffee to a new height. The first two civilizations are where the brand stands and looks. The third is where the brand places itself.

The frame did not stay on paper.

On the morning of June 16, 2020, the date Trung Nguyen still takes as its birthday, an energy coffee garden built around the three civilizations opened.

At the space at 12 Alexandre de Rhodes in District One, a performance of the three coffee civilizations was staged with light, music, and 3D mapping; that program was later moved to the World Coffee Museum The Tao of Coffee.

The entire retail and drinks range at the stores was reorganized under the three groups. Three words became a menu, packaging, brewing equipment, the arrangement of tables and chairs.

In November 2023 a forty-five-minute documentary, The Tao of Coffee, produced by Trung Nguyen Legend in collaboration with Warner Bros. Discovery, was broadcast on the Discovery Channel in Australia and New Zealand on the twenty-fourth, and in Vietnam, South Korea and Japan on the thirtieth.

It was filmed in Buon Ma Thuot and at the World Coffee Museum.

For a brand about to step outside the border, this matters more than it appears. To say Vietnamese coffee is to begin the story with a product, and a product is immediately set against products that have been there a long time. To say three coffee civilizations is to begin with a frame, and inside that frame Vietnam is not the latecomer but the holder of one of the three places.

It is the same move played at the Reunification Palace

in 2003, when the cups were brought out with no labels. That time it was removing the name in order to compare taste. This time it is changing the field of comparison altogether: not who is better, but what coffee is.

The price of the move is higher too. A product only has to be put on a shelf. An idea has to find someone willing to receive it, and that someone is sitting in a city that already has its own way of drinking coffee and its own familiar names. He has a few minutes for a cup, and there is no assurance he wants to hear anything more.

In 2023 a store named Trung Nguyen Legend opened in Westminster, California, in the middle of a large Vietnamese community. Then San Jose. Then Portland, Philadelphia, Houston, Beaverton. Each name is one stretch further from Little Saigon, and in those places the question is no longer whether Americans will drink Vietnamese coffee.

The question is whether they will step into the story.

From Buon Ma Thuot to California is twenty-seven years and half the world. But the hardest distance to cross may be no longer than a table: from the cup set down in front of a person, to the point where that person decides to come back again.

PART FIVE

The Road to America

2022–2026 · Chapters 23–27

An avenue in Westminster where Vietnamese people have lived for fifty years. A shop on Bellaire that took four years to open after the lease was signed. A number announced, and a number that can be counted.

Thirty years after an application was signed in Buon Ma Thuot, the road that carried a family away from the sea is still there, and it still carries coffee.

CHAPTER 23

Nearly Fifty Years of Coffee Before the Shop

The First Shop on American Ground

9039 Bolsa Avenue, Westminster, California. Thirteen hundred square feet, open from seven in the morning to five in the afternoon. Inside there are phin filters, an espresso machine, wooden trays, egg coffee and weasel coffee. The beans come from Buon Ma Thuot.

That was the first Trung Nguyen Legend shop on American ground.

Not New York, not central Los Angeles, not San Francisco. A street in the middle of Little Saigon, where Vietnamese is still spoken on the sidewalk and the signs are still in two languages.
That street has a history of its own, and it is longer than the history of the name that had just set foot on it.

In the mid-1970s Westminster was a town of about sixty thousand, with a few machine shops and mostly farmland: strawberry fields, orange groves, plant nurseries. Both sides of Bolsa were thinly built then. In every season there were black furrows and a row of people bent over picking. There was more country in the air than city.

In 1975, some fifty thousand Vietnamese arrived in Southern California and were housed temporarily at Camp Pendleton. Once the paperwork was done, churches across Orange County sponsored many of them and brought them north, under an hour's drive. Housing was cheaper, work easier to find, the weather easier to take. People stayed.

The first businesses carried very familiar names: Mr. Danh's pharmacy, the Quê Hương market, the Hòa Bình market, the Thanh Mỹ restaurant. In the early 1980s, by the account of people who were there, several men and women working in machine shops pooled their wages to rent a small unit as a place to gather. It was called a center, but it held only tables and chairs, a few books, and free weekend classes: English, electronics, help filling out forms, and even classes in printed-circuit design taught by volunteer Vietnamese engineers. On weekdays the door stayed shut. On Saturday and Sunday, Vietnamese came out of it into the street.

Alongside those places, restaurants opened. And in every restaurant there was coffee.

That is the detail most easily missed in this chapter. Vietnamese who came to America brought with them the habit of a glass of iced milk coffee in the morning, brought the familiar bitterness and the familiar smell after a shift. Filter coffee was on Bolsa Avenue before that street had its name on any map.

Then the name arrived. By 1986 there were more than five hundred Vietnamese-owned businesses around Bolsa. One of the first to call the area Little Saigon was the newspaper Sàigòn Nhỏ, founded in 1985. In 1987 the Asian Garden Mall was built. On June 17, 1988, Governor George Deukmejian signed the recognition of the area as a commercial and tourist district, and had highway signs bearing the words "Little Saigon" put up on Interstate 405 and State Route 22. Thirteen signs, for an area whose boundaries were written into the document: Westminster Boulevard, Bolsa Avenue, Magnolia Street, Euclid Street.

Thirty-seven years later, on April 18, 2025, the stretch of the 405 between Bolsa Avenue and Bolsa Chica Street was named the Little Saigon Freeway. The signs were paid for by private contributions.

From strawberry rows to a name on a federal highway is fifty years, and nobody handed that distance to anybody.

That is the street a coffee brand from Buon Ma Thuot stepped onto in 2023.

The franchisee was H&L Wholesale Food Corporation, a company based in Los Angeles. The company was no stranger to the name Trung Nguyen: it had been the distributor of Trung Nguyen's packaged coffee in the United States. Jennie Tang, its chief executive, said what they wanted to bring over was not a drink but the business of sitting down together. The shop opened on September 21. The formal opening was on October 1, crowded enough that customers stood waiting for a table. Two days for one beginning, as there had been twenty-seven years earlier in Buon Ma Thuot.

The photo backdrop that day was a portrait of Napoleon on horseback, and Napoleon's line about coffee was printed on the service ware.

In the middle of Little Saigon, the brand laid out exactly what it had built at home: coffee as part of European history, of great names, of a civilization rather than a glass of liquid.

Ms. Tang explained the numbering on the menu: the higher the number, the more premium the coffee, number 1 being pure robusta, heavy and high in caffeine, numbers 3 and 5 pure arabica. Alongside the phin and the egg coffee, this branch alone added cold brew and iced egg coffee — two items for the local palate.

This was not the arrival of Vietnamese coffee in America. Vietnamese coffee had been on that street for nearly fifty years, in every pho house, in every small restaurant. Even the name had come first: G7 entered the Costco and E-mart retail systems in early October 2011. Many of the people standing in line that day had been drinking Trung Nguyen for more than ten years, bought in American supermarkets, and only that day saw an actual shop.

What was new lay elsewhere. A Vietnamese brand entered the United States through the door of its own community.

That door opens more easily than any other. The customers already knew the name, already knew the taste, needed no one to explain what a phin was. But the door that opens easily is also a narrow one, because a community is only so large, and a name already familiar is hard to be surprised by.

By the time the Westminster shop opened, Trung Nguyen Legend had four factories and a hundred and ten shops in Vietnam, along with three in China — where the brand had gone abroad for the first time in September 2022, opening at the Taikoo Hui mall at 699 West Nanjing Road in Shanghai. Thirteen hundred square feet on Bolsa Avenue was the first point of a different test.

From Little Saigon the road continued. San Jose. Portland. Philadelphia. Houston.

And the question left on Bolsa Avenue is still there: is a brand entering the United States through the door of its own community selling coffee to Vietnamese, or borrowing Vietnamese as a step up to somewhere else?

The answer is not in the first shop. The answer is in the shops that come after.

CHAPTER 24

Four Years Between a Signature and an Opening Day

Bellaire

Bellaire Boulevard, Houston, Texas. Signs in Vietnamese, Chinese, and English crowd each other for miles. In the morning the smell of pho and the smell of coffee mix into the sound of engines.

On March 21, 2026, at number 11754 on that road, a space called Trung Nguyen Legend World Coffee opened. Four thousand seven hundred square feet, about a hundred and thirty seats. It had been in soft opening since March 10.

The figure of four thousand seven hundred is worth a pause. The first shop on Bolsa Avenue three years earlier was thirteen hundred square feet. This is more than three times that, and the difference is not one of area. Thirteen hundred square feet is a place to pour coffee and pass it across a counter. Four thousand seven hundred square feet with a hundred and thirty chairs is a place for people to stay.

Staying requires a reason to stay. That is where the three coffee civilizations — Ottoman, Roman, and Zen — were built out, in a space the group describes as carrying the marks of Vietnamese culture. The frame set out in Buon Ma Thuot and Saigon was carried to a boulevard in Texas almost intact.

But the most substantial part of this chapter is not in the press release.

The two people who built the shop are Vietnamese living there. They signed the lease on that space in 2022. The shop opened in March 2026.

Four years.
Between a signature and an opening day, for a commercial space in the United States, lie permits,

drawings, electrical and plumbing systems, fire inspection, and ventilation for a four-thousand-seven-hundred-square-foot room. And months in which the rent runs while the door stays shut. The people who signed in 2022 did not know what year the door would open.

This is the distinction that has to be made plainly, because the usual phrasing in the press misleads.

Trung Nguyen did not open a shop in Houston. Trung Nguyen supplied the name, the model, the formula, and the goods. The rent, the construction, the wages, and those four years of waiting belonged to two people in Houston.

Earlier on the same Bellaire corridor there had been a Trung Nguyen E-Coffee outlet, the fast model, buy and go. Now on the same road there is the opposite model. One sells a few minutes; the other sells a few hours.

The group called March 21, 2026, the opening of its tenth franchised shop in the United States.

Bellaire, like Bolsa, is a street of the community. So the question left in Westminster three years earlier comes back here, and this time it is larger along with the floor area: are a hundred and thirty chairs on a street that already has Vietnamese on it a place to serve that community, or a place for other people to see?

Four years between a signature and an opening day says that somebody has bet the answer is worth waiting for.

CHAPTER 25

The Number Announced and the Number Counted

A Hundred Shops

In the release of March 21, 2026, reprinted almost word for word by many newspapers, the group set out a target of a hundred shops in the United States, about a hundred and thirty in China, and plans to expand into Melbourne, Canada, India, Japan, South Korea, Dubai, and France. A hundred is a round number, and this book has met round numbers before.

In 2006, G7 Mart was announced with nine thousand five hundred points of sale. In 2012, a book program was announced with a hundred million copies, in a country of some ninety million people. Fourteen years later, the figure the group announces for books given away is more than five million. The number announced and the number counted are two different things. Both belong to this company's record, and dropping either one bends the story to one side.

The number announced states an ambition and makes people pay attention. The number counted states the real speed of a business. Three years between Bolsa and Bellaire produced ten shops, by the group's own count.

That count also needs stating clearly, because the system has several models. There is Trung Nguyen Legend. There is Trung Nguyen Legend World Coffee.

There is E-Coffee, the small fast model. Depending on which models are included, the figure comes out differently, and reports in the same year do not always carry the same number.

But there is something the multiplication from ten to a hundred does not say.

Each of those ten is a lease, in the name of a person

or a group of people on the ground. In Westminster it was a distribution company in Los Angeles. In Houston it was two people who waited four years. The group supplies the name and the model; the capital sits on the other side.

A hundred shops in the United States, therefore, is not a hundred decisions made by a company in Buon Ma Thuot. It is a hundred other people willing to sign, willing to pay rent through the months the door is shut, and willing to believe the name will sell in their city. Ninety more people have to think what the two in Houston thought.

While the figure of a hundred is being repeated, new outlets keep opening in the ordinary way. On August 9, 2026, an E-Coffee opened in Garland, Texas. There is no summing-up article for a shop like that. There is only one more name on a list, and one more owner opening the door at seven in the morning.

On June 16, 2026, thirty years were counted again from Buon Ma Thuot.

By then the question was no longer whether a hundred shops would be reached. The question was what those thirty years had produced that is not counted in shops.

CHAPTER 26

From Nguyen Kiem to Nguyen Hue

Thirty Years

68 Nguyen Hue, Ho Chi Minh City.

In the evening the walking street is crowded. Children run down the middle of the road, people photograph themselves in front of old buildings, and light from the shopfronts falls onto the stone. This is the most expensive address in one of the largest cities in Southeast Asia.

On June 16, 2026,
a Trung Nguyen Legend World Coffee space opened there, marking thirty years from June 16, 1996. Those thirty years are counted from a date the company chose for itself. The licence carries the date of August 15.

The sixty days before it were when a few friends started work, that is the day taken as the birthday. Thirty years on, the choice still stands.

Twenty-eight years earlier, the first time this name came down to Saigon, the address was 587 Nguyen Kiem, and the way it opened was to give coffee away for ten days, just after losing all its capital in Long Xuyen. Nguyen Kiem then was not an address anybody knew.

From Nguyen Kiem to Nguyen Hue is twenty-eight years and about six kilometers in the same city.

That month was not only Nguyen Hue. On June 6, a space of the same kind opened at 52 Truong Dinh. Ten days before that, on May 30, an E-Coffee opened in Katy, Texas. The plan for June and July also held Huntington Beach in California and Beaverton in Oregon.

A thirty-year-old name opening on a walking street in Saigon and in a Texas suburb in the same summer.

Inside the space on Nguyen Hue are the familiar things: the three coffee civilizations, the wooden trays, the brewing sets, and beans from Buon Ma Thuot. A person walking in off the street may know nothing about any of it. They order a glass, sit down, look out at the road. The coffee is brewed, the money is paid, the glass is cleared.

Thirty years ago, the same motions, in an entirely different place: a drum turned by hand, fired with wood, in a highland town, with a few kilos of coffee taken on credit and a bicycle for making deliveries.

The distance between those two scenes is the whole content of this book.

CHAPTER 27

Three Lines That Do Not Meet

What Has Not Been Closed

On the business application of August 15, 1996, there were the names of several friends.

By the registration of change dated November 27, 2000, the list carries the name of Mr. Vu's father, and no friend's name at all.

The four years between those two papers are the four most important years of a young business: opening the shop in Saigon, the ten free days, the first deliveries, the nights when everyone still had to carry the goods himself. No document records what they did in those four years, when they left, or why.

They are not the only ones.

The family that lent two hundred million in 1996 has no name in any account. Neither does the woman with the shop in Tuy Hoa, who gave a few students their first roasting formula. Neither does the partner in Long Xuyen, where the capital was lost.

A business keeps papers about what it owns. Nobody opens a file on the people who helped.

That is where a book about thirty years has to stop and say so plainly: not everything is recorded, and what is recorded tends to be what has legal standing. Money leaves receipts. Shares leave a register. A promise to hand over coffee on credit leaves nothing.

Thirty years also do not close the three lines running in parallel through this story.

The first is a person. Out of Ninh Hoa up to M'Drak, from the medical lecture hall to the roasting drum, from a man selling coffee to a public figure, then to a farm on the plateau and the years of appearing rarely.

The second is a name. From a household business to a cooperative, to a limited company, to a joint-stock company, to a group of legal persons the coffee drinker never sees, and then out to Shanghai, to Bolsa, to Bellaire.

The third is an idea. Coffee as a drink, then as a Vietnamese brand, then as energy and creativity, then as books given away, then as three civilizations.

The three set off from the same place in 1996. Thirty years later they stand in three different places, and they do not lie on top of each other at any point.

The person has withdrawn to somewhere quiet. The name is on the Nguyen Hue walking street and on a boulevard in Texas. The idea is inside books handed out at border posts and in lecture halls.

Anyone who reads this story has to arrange those three lines for himself.

The most certain thing in the whole book is still the

thing from the first page.

In 1979 a family left Ngoc Diem, on the road that joins the sea to the highlands, bringing a child with them. That road took them away from the sea, into the red earth, to a place whose name nobody knew.

On that land in Ngoc Diem there is now an ancestral hall built by Mr. Vu. The recorder saw it there; no document about it has been found.

Thirty years after the child raised a name, the road is still there, and it still carries coffee. Only the direction has changed.

Now the goods go from the highlands out to the sea, and then onward.

CLOSING

This book was assembled, not composed.

What was available was read: newspaper articles from 2004 and 2007, court reporting from 2019, a company history page, business filings, trade statistics, franchise announcements, a shopfront on an avenue in California, a road in Khanh Hoa. What was available was placed in order of time. Where two records disagreed, both were left standing.

Nothing has been added to make the sequence flow better. There are places in these chapters where the reader will feel a hand reaching for the next event and finding nothing there. Those gaps are accurate.

A recorder is not a biographer. A biographer explains a life; the explanation is what the reader buys. A recorder sets down what can be shown and stops at the edge of it, and the reader does the rest of the work himself. That is a less satisfying book to read and a more honest one to leave behind.

Thirty years is a round number. The people in this story did not live in round numbers. They lived in kilos, in days of rent, in batches ruined and batches saved, in the distance between a promise made on Monday and the money handed over on Friday.

Those are the things that were counted here.
The rest was not claimed.

WHAT REMAINS OPEN

The following are unresolved in the sources consulted for this book. They are listed so that a reader who finds an answer knows exactly what he has found.

The year he entered university. The 2004 first-person account gives 1990. Vietnamese Wikipedia and several biographical files give 1992. Other articles give his age as twenty, which spans February 1991 to February 1992. No school document has been located.

What happened to his studies.

The sources support two things: that he was urged to return to school, and that he returned. Whether he continued, and whether he graduated, is not established anywhere. All sources agree only that he did not practice medicine.

Two million dong, and when.
One set of articles from 2007 and 2008 places the sum at age sixteen. A later account, quoting the original newspaper, places it at age ten. The two readings fall on opposite sides of the 1985 currency exchange, so they are not the same sum of money.

The woman in Tuy Hoa.
No source records her name. What she gave away in one afternoon is in the record; she is not.

The lending family.
Two hundred million dong was borrowed in 1996 from a family that no source names, and repaid, by his testimony, at twenty-five million a month for twenty-three years.

How many friends signed.
The 1996 application is described in some accounts as bearing four names and in others as bearing five. This book does not choose.

Two founding dates.
June 16 and August 15, 1996, sixty days apart, both in circulation, both used by the company at different times.

The year the Creative range appeared.
The company's own history page does not mention it. No source consulted gives a launch year.

How many shops in the United States.
One figure has been announced and another can be counted, and the two do not match.

Announced targets.
Nine thousand five hundred points of sale, and one hundred million books to be given away, were stated as goals. No independent count of either has been located.

The night journey from Tuy Hoa.

The return trip appears in accounts the recorder was given, but no published source confirms it.

Ninh Hoa or Hoa Vang.

Published sources give Ninh Hoa as the place of birth. At least one reference work gives Hoa Vang, Da Nang, as the ancestral home. These are two different claims and are often merged into one.

The ancestral hall at Ngoc Diem.

The recorder saw it. No document about it has been found.

CHRONOLOGY

Entries marked (announced) are figures or events stated by the company. Entries marked (disputed) appear differently in different sources.

1857 / 1908 — Arabica, then robusta, introduced to Vietnam.

1922 — The CADA estate, about 2,000 hectares, among the large plantations of the highlands.

1971, February 10 — Dang Le Nguyen Vu born, Khanh Hoa province.

1975 — Vietnam has roughly 13,000 hectares of coffee.

1979 — A family leaves Ngoc Diem for M'Drak.

1985, September 14 — Currency exchange, one new dong for ten old.

1986 — Roughly 50,000 hectares under coffee.

1988 / 1993 — Resolution 10, then the Land Law: the mechanisms that put land into households' hands.

1990 — Enters the medical faculty, Tay Nguyen University (disputed: 1990 / 1991 / 1992).

1995, January 21 — Buon Ma Thuot becomes a city.

1996, June 16 or August 15 — Trung Nguyen founded in Buon Ma Thuot (disputed).

1998, August — First coffee shop in Saigon, 587 Nguyen Kiem, Phu Nhuan.

1999, July 19 — Trung Nguyen Coffee Enterprise Cooperative.

2000 — Hanoi.

2001 — Franchises in Japan and Singapore; the slogan Khoi nguon sang tao announced (announced).

2002, December 2 — Trung Nguyen Coffee Company Limited.

2003, November 23 — Blind tasting at the Reunification Palace; G7 launched.

2006, April 12 — Joint-stock structure registered.

2006 — G7 Mart announced: about 500 stores, a target of 9,500 points of sale (announced).

2009 — The horse project on the Krong A hills.

2010 — Exports stated to more than sixty countries (announced).

2012 — The Journey of Great Ambition; one hundred million books announced (announced).

2015 — A civil matter begins; it runs six years.

2016 — Twentieth anniversary; Trung Nguyen Legend

Café; two million books stated as given (announced). In October, King Coffee launches in the United States.

2017 — Representative office, Shanghai.

2018 — World Coffee Museum opens; the Trung Nguyen Legend brand introduced.

2021 — The civil matter concludes.

2022, September 21 — First shop outside Vietnam: Taikoo Hui, 699 West Nanjing Road, Shanghai.

2023 — First shop on American ground, 9039 Bolsa Avenue, Westminster, California; twenty years of G7; representative office, South Korea.

2024 — San Jose: Story Road, then Capitol Expressway.

2025 — Portland. Ground broken on a plant in Dak Lak. On July 1, Ninh Ich merges into Nam Ninh Hoa.

2026, March 10 and 21 — Soft opening and opening, Bellaire, Houston.

June 16 — the Nguyen Hue space, Ho Chi Minh City.

August 9 — E-Coffee, Garland, Texas.

SOURCES, BY CHAPTER

Chapters 1–4 — Red Earth. Provincial and national coffee statistics 1975–2000. Founding documents of Tay Nguyen University, Decision 298-CP (1977). Decree 08-CP (1995) on the status of Buon Ma Thuot. Currency and wage instruments of 1985 and 1988. The 2004 first-person account. What the recorder was told at Ngoc Diem in August 2026.

Chapters 5–8 — The Roasting Drum. The 2004 first-person account; articles of 2007 and 2008 carrying the same material. Trade production figures for 1994–1996. The formula received at Tuy Hoa is recorded as an account, not as a document.

Chapters 9–15 — When the Name Begins. Testimony given by the parties at the 2019 hearing, as reported. Business registration records for 1996 and 2006. The company's own history page for 1998, 2000, 2001 and 2003. Reporting on the November 23, 2003 tasting, including the participation figure announced by the organizer.

Chapters 16–22 — The Ecosystem. Company announcements 2006–2022. Press coverage of the title coffee king, recorded as press usage and not as a conferred title. Shareholder records of 2014. Four dated documents for the years 2015–2021, and no narration of proceedings.

Chapters 23–27 — The Road to America. Franchise and opening announcements; local press for Westminster, San Jose, Portland, Philadelphia, Houston, Beaverton and Garland; addresses and opening dates as published. Shop counts are given both as announced and as counted, and the difference is left standing.

Photographs and on-site observation at Ngoc Diem and Ninh Hoa, Khanh Hoa, in August 2026, each recorded with date and hour.

ACKNOWLEDGMENTS

This book was read before it was printed, and it is better for it.

Two editors went through the manuscript chapter by chapter. One of them kept asking where a sentence stopped being a fact and started being a conclusion, and the question improved almost every page. The other checked numbers against the documents that produced them, and found several that could not survive the check.

A rule came out of that work and stayed: if the answer to "how do we know this" is "because it makes sense," the sentence has to be looked at again. Whatever is still standing in these chapters has been through it.

Thanks are owed to the people at Ngoc Diem who answered questions from a stranger with a notebook, and to those in Ninh Hoa who pointed out the road.

The errors that remain belong to the recorder.

Note: personal names and any institution the author wishes to thank go here, in this order — editors, readers, people on the ground, family. The paragraphs above are written to accept names without rewriting.

ABOUT THE RECORDER

A person who writes a book is usually called an author. **Calvin P. Tran** chose another word: the **Recorder**.

Under the pen name **Từ Yên** he began writing in the summer of 1972, in Vietnam. The work withdrew for years and returned without warning — Palawan in 1979, San Jose in 1980, Saigon in September 1990. It did not become more frequent, only more inward.

His books are records rather than arguments: Trump, a Curious Tale, Night 1002 — The Persian Dawn, AMERICA: The Stillness, WORLD: Fracture Lines...

Trung Nguyên Coffee is the first of them about a business.

He lives in the United States.

Counted. Not Claimed.

Also by

TRAN BOOKS

WORLD: Fracture Lines

Writing. Responsibility.

The world rarely changes all at once.
More often, it changes through fractures.

Library of Congress Control Number: 2026918722
ISBN: 979-8-9958530-7-7 | Also available as an eBook.

Trump, a Curious Tale

Record. Not Judge.

On spectacle, power, and the emotional
architecture of modern politics.

Library of Congress Control Number: 2026903064
ISBN: 979-8-9958530-0-8 | Also available as an eBook.

Trump, Kỳ truyện

Record. Not Judge.

On spectacle, power, and the emotional
architecture of modern politics.

Library of Congress Control Number: 2026903064
ISBN: 979-8-9958530-1-5 | Also available as an eBook.

Night 1002 — The Persian Dawn

Witness. Write. Endure.

Where empires continue speaking
after history believes the story has ended.

Library of Congress Control Number: 2026910703
ISBN: 979-8-9958530-2-2 | Also available as an eBook.

AMERICA: *The Stillness*

Silence. Records.

A chronicle written through silence rather than declaration.

Library of Congress Control Number: 2026913471
ISBN: 979-8-9958530-8-4 | Also available as an eBook.

Where Havana Goes

Asked. Not Answered.

Ninety miles, and one hundred twenty-eight years, 1898–2026.

Library of Congress Control Number: 2026923022
ISBN: 979-8-9977742-1-9 | Also available as an eBook.

Musk & Trump

Dated. Not Decided.

Didn't Need Each Other. Needed Each Other.
Tore Into Each Other. Shook Hands Again.

Library of Congress Control Number: 2026923090
ISBN: 979-8-9977742-2-6 | Also available as an eBook.

Trung Nguyen Coffee

Counted. Not Claimed.

Thirty Years of a Name, 1996–2026

Library of Congress Control Number: 2026921623
ISBN: 979-8-9958530-6-0 | Also available as an eBook.

Amazon: amazon.com/author/calvinptran

Goodreads: goodreads.com/tranbooks

Publisher: tranbooks.com

www.ingramcontent.com/pod-product-compliance
Lightning Source LLC
LaVergne TN
LVHW100730061126
851857LV00011B/473